To Lira
Love grandma Bee
+ grandpa

Evelyn 2019

For Pearl, Rocket, Sparky & Boy-D;

three large, loving, licking, loony Labrador Retrievers

& a Jack Russell 'Terrorist'.

My first pack.

Three Bad Labs

Story & Illustrations
Evangelia Philippidis

We are three bad labs and we're OK.

we play all night,

we sleep all day.

We eat your lunch,

we chew your shoes,

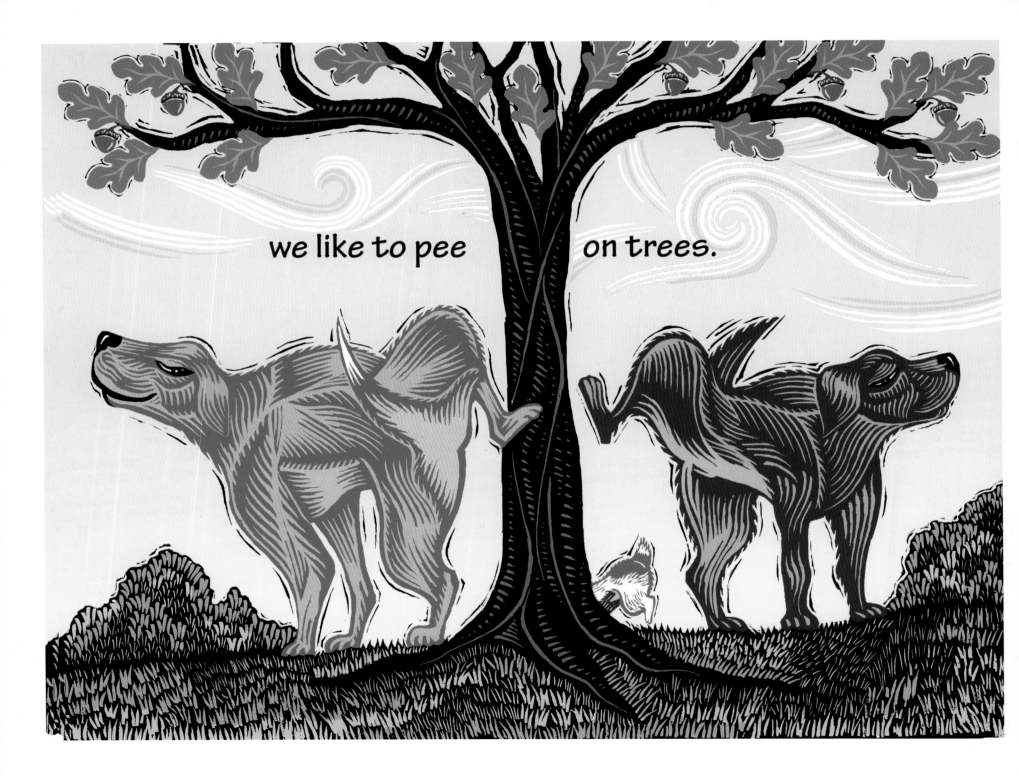

On weekends we go swimming,
swan diving if we please.

We are three bad labs and we're OK.

We howl all night.

we shed all day.

We chase the cats,

we sniff our butts,

We love our brother Boy-D,
we found him
in the park

We are three bad labs and we're OK.

We follow you
all night,

we wait for you all day.

We fetch your ducks,

we shred your socks,

and your mother's finest lace.

ABOVE: Boy-D, a sweet, lost soul with lots of heart and a drive to run.

LEFT: From left to right, Rocket, Sparky & Pearl, the best Bad Labs in the world.

Acknowledgements

Many thanks...

To my husband Bob, who on Christmas day 1995, lovingly presented me with three incredible souls that changed my life forever. In 2003 he had the great heart to save Boy-D, three hours before he was to be put down.

To Cheryl, who bred and nurtured great Labrador Retrievers and taught me all the things that were good and not so good about raising dogs.

To Gary J, who during a food and wine induced sing-a-long started the inspiration wheels turning.

To my family and friends, from Greece to Australia, Lorain to West Jefferson, Ohio and my students at CCAD, who encouraged me to fulfill the dream of writing and illustrating this book.

About Evangelia

Born and raised in Athens, Greece, Evangelia Philippidis
immigrated to the United states in 1966.

As a full-time Designer/Illustrator for The Columbus Dispatch for
22 years, Evangelia's award-winning work was featured regularly
on its pages. Editorial illustration is perfectly suited to her
scratchboard technique and her penchant for storytelling
(a favorite Greek pastime).

She is adjunct instructor of illustration at The Columbus College
of Art & Design, and is nationally recognized for her work.

She lives in Columbus, Ohio with her husband Bob James, Boy-D the
old Jack Russell Terrier, Maggie , the big red dog, Petey, the punked
out Chihuahua and Panda, the chunky Chug.

In her ongoing effort to help animals in need, a portion of the sales of
this book are donated to the Friends of the Shelter. The Columbus
based non profit organization raises funds for the veterinary care
and adoption efforts of sick and injured dogs at the Franklin County
Dog Shelter, in Columbus, Ohio.

To see more of her work go to www.therartofevangelia.net